SHATTERED TRUST

A Story of Incest

Kristine Barnard

"To the child who hid from me the truth for all these years. I can only say she has grown into a wonderful and strong woman."

Table of Contents

Author's Other Book

"Screw Breast Cancer Awareness Month. Take Action
Now The New Mantra: The Controversial Rantings Of
A Breast Cancer Survivor."

August 2020

Introduction

WHEN I STARTED this book, I was filled with many questions. I imagine I could fill a textbook and tell this story with just the questions I need to ask. Sadly, there will be no answers to my questions, as there is no one left to interrogate.

How do you begin a story of this nature? How can I reveal the story that has been buried deep in my soul for many long years? How can I expose myself to others, not knowing how they will feel about me? I am frightened to reveal the truth.

After years of being buried alive, the events of that summer have clawed their way free from the hole where they lay hidden.

It is a true story, a truth that begs to be released, for the child inside who lived it and for the others out there who have suffered in silence as well. May they, too, find the courage to tell their stories of lost trust and release the demons that have surely tried to devour them.

Rape, incest, and molestation happen all the time to many innocent victims.

Those weaker are at the mercy of the fiends who will use them.

As in the serenity prayer I ask, "God give me the strength, courage and wisdom" to tell my story, to give strength to others, and the courage for all victims to release their stories to the world.

God grant me, whatever it takes to free the child of these hauntings.

PART I:
Childhood
(Before that Summer)

Chapter One

THE MEMORIES COME uninvited like flashes of lightning bursting through a window during a storm. Great explosions of light highlight those within. The people in the room seem mere shadows, indistinguishable, but highlighted, just as my memories are highlighted when they pierce the darkness that is my memory.

I am seventy now. I can hardly believe so much time has passed. How many times have these memories screamed through my brain like the winds of a hurricane?

Great flashes of memories setting my heart ablaze come uninvited to the forefront of my thoughts to invade my moment of peace.

I do not ask for the reminders. I do not wish to remember, but the story slithers out of its hiding place to wrap me in sadness yet again.

When I think back to the events, I compare them to other stories I have heard. Horrendous stories of rape and torture, and I think mine do not sound so tragic. Not nearly as gruesome as so many.

I think others might feel my trauma is not as traumatic as those others. It did not go on for years, just one summer, but that summer was enough to shatter the innocence of an eight-year-old for the rest of her days. And so, the story unfolds.

My earliest childhood recollections are harmless, full of fun and laughter. I cannot list my memories by date or time, they just float up to my consciousness like little bubbles, bouncing from one thing to another.

I will admit that I was a skinny little kid, gregarious and full of vim and vigor as they used to say. I was the third child. The clown. Always bringing a smile or laugh to the adults. I felt safe in the cockiness that came from feeling loved and cared for.

We were a happy family, I think. I do not have memories of my parents ranting and raving at each other. Not until after that summer. I do not have memories of fights or curse words.

My mother worked as a waitress because my father's work was unreliable. He came home from the navy without any special skills, so he painted houses, inside and out, as well as businesses. Often, he was gone for long hours of the day to return late at night. He'd go weeks on end without a pay check until the job was finished.

There are happy memories, and memories of struggling as our family worked to survive the hard times.

One thing I do remember quite well is that we were extremely poor. There were days when all I had to eat were sugar sandwiches because the cupboards were bare.

I would slather a big glob of butter onto some bread, and then smear a couple of huge teaspoons of sugar all around, and snarf it down.

Sometimes, I would wolf down two or three sandwiches, depending on how much bread was in the house. It was always feast or famine, depending on the sporadic paychecks of my father, and the tips my mother earned as a waitress. In my memories most of the time I see me, not the others.

I remember spooning peanut butter right out of the jar. It tasted wonderful. Satisfying. A couple of spoons of that creamy stuff knocked the hunger right out of my gut, at least for a little while.

Sometimes my mother would come home with a bag full of chili burgers, bought on credit at the local restaurant, and we would devour them like a pack of ravenous dogs, gagging and choking as we hurried to fill our bellies. They were so damn good.

I felt shame when the local store owner glared when I would come in with my shopping list in hand from my mother, expecting credit yet again. Sometimes I returned home empty handed with my head hanging because he said, "Not this time. Not till you pay the bill."

Our electricity got disconnected many times. The gas, too. Once when I was a teenager, there were weeks when I would run a garden hose from my neighbor's basement taps to our bathroom so I could take a hot bath. No gas, no heat, no hot water. There were no organizations preventing families from freezing to death from lack of heat in the winter then.

We lived in a duplex and the utilities were separated. One side could be turned off if the bill wasn't paid, while the other remained on.

I would drag the hose from the basement clear up to our bathroom. I was the only one of my siblings who cared about a hot bath.

The upstairs couple were friends of mine as I would babysit for them off and on, and in turn they allowed me to use their hot water along with the few dollars they gave me for spending money. I am sure they pitied me hauling that disgusting snake of a hose upstairs just so I could bathe.

Chapter Two

I HAVE RECOLLECTIONS of washing my clothes by hand in the basement, the water so cold my fingers would go numb, and wringing them out with our old wringer washing machine, afraid it would crush my fingers as I pushed the clothes through the spinning, grinding wringers. It took days for those clothes to dry in that fricking cold basement.

We never owned a washer or dryer. The old wringer washer did not wash, it only wrung out the clothes. Sadly, it was my sister and I who did the laundry most days. I remember the humiliation of hauling our dirty laundry down the street in our wagon to the local laundromat, hoping no one would see us.

What a chore when there were six in my family. Pillowcases (as there were no extra strong Glad bags) full of dirty clothes tumbling off the wagon as we trudged down the street.

Just yesterday on Facebook someone posted pictures of the old wringer washing machines I grew up using, asking who knew what these were. What a joke on me! There were several children who had gotten broken fingers or arms from getting caught in those wretched wringers as they squashed the clothes and their limbs. The machines were too treacherous for a child to use, and yet we did anyway.

We moved from neighborhood to neighborhood because my parents often could not pay the rent. Eviction was a common occurrence. My folks always tried to stay in the same school district because there was only one Catholic school, and we were good little Catholics.

Sometimes word got out to the local homeowners who rented homes, and no one would rent to our family. Shameful is what it was, especially when my father always had money for beer.

My parents were worker bees. Neither had received any kind of education. My mother made it through grade school. My father joined the Canadian navy before he met my mother, and then the children tumbled out.

The American navy would not take him because he had a limp left over from a bout of childhood polio. The Canadians were not so picky. He was only in for a year or two before they were married, and there were no veteran benefits after discharge in those days. Poor or not.

I have a picture of my parents out at a club somewhere. My father in his navy uniform and mom in a dress with makeup in place. Both looked so grown up although they were only teenagers. My mother just seventeen. They looked stunning, just like movie stars.

Sadly, my mother was never afforded the pleasure of a high school education (at least not until she was in her fifties). She was smart as a whip, but never had a chance to put it to good use. Marriage and motherhood were her shackles.

None of my siblings or first cousins ever received a college education. Attending college and earning a degree in any field were goals "only rich people" could afford.

There were no Pell grants, or student loans for those without the finances who craved further education. I was the first, and that did not happen until I was in my fifties just like my mother. But things were not always gloomy at our house.

As a family we played lots of games. We kids were easily entertained. I could play poker by age nine, craps by ten, and pinochle by eleven. Board games like Monopoly, royal rummy, and gin were also great time fillers.

Television was almost non-existent clicking off at a set time until morning. Can you imagine no programs to put you to sleep? No shopping!

Nothing except for a blank screen, and the spooky flicker of static. Sometimes, you could hear voices bleeding through from some distant channel. Think the Poltergeist movie and ghostly whispers. That was our television.

Cable had not yet been invented. The rabbit ear antenna strength was so weak that sometimes all you got was an ear-piercing buzzing sound or a nauseating, blurred picture.

I remember moving to Kansas and discovering that people "paid" for television. I was appalled. Pay for television?

The best times though were the hours I spent outside playing and roaming the neighborhood. As I said, I was a gregarious child and loved to talk to people, often I would visit the local shop owners and talk their heads off if they were not busy. I do not recall the conversations, but I always felt safe and welcomed in their stores.

One local grocery would let me stamp the canned goods and put them on the shelves. I loved it. The sound of that stamper clapping the cans and marking them with a price is still fresh in my brain. I felt so grown up. Sometimes, I was rewarded with a free candy bar or two. Those were real treasures.

My favorite place to meander was a local music shop. I loved to wander the aisles, lightly brushing my fingertips across the instruments as I chatted with the fellow who owned the shop.

I yearned to learn to play the piano. I loved its cool,

clean white and black keys, but music lessons and instruments were not in my future. No money for that sort of thing.

This wonderful man allowed me to tap on the piano, pluck the strings of a nearby guitar, or just sit and watch him string bows out of horse tail.

I could not get over the fact that they cut off a horse's tail to make strings for bows. He assured me that they did not take the whole tail, and it did not hurt the horse. As an adult, I am more aware of slaughterhouses and things of that nature. Poor babies.

I was surprised as I ran those hairs through my fingers and noticed how coarse they felt. How could these bristly strands make such lovely music? And the scent of the wood cleaner perfuming the air was heaven to my nose. Lemon and a little something else dancing in the air.

Another great family adventure was the drive-in theater. My mother just loved a night out. We would go in our pajamas, play on the playground until dark, and then fall asleep while she got to watch the movies in peace.

She loved the new movies that played on the big screen. All that color just dazzled the eye. At home, the only choice was a black and white screen. It was years before we could afford a color television.

So, for a few bucks, the whole family got a movie, cartoons, and popcorn. It was a cheap night out that was enjoyed by all. Funny, I do not remember my father ever going with us to the drive-in.

Chapter Three

My siblings and I were not alone in the world. We had a slew of cousins just across the river in Windsor, Ontario. My grandparents and all our extended family lived just across the border.

Visits were a common occurrence as there was not much else to do. Mom worked nights tending bar, which left a lot of free time for my dad, so off we would go to grandmother's house. Dad could guzzle booze with the grownups, and we got to play with our cousins.

There were two ways to cross the border. One was driving through a dark, dank tunnel that ran under the Detroit River from end to end. Or you could travel across the long, rickety old bridge.

In our nightmares either way you were risking sudden death. One being crushed to death as the tunnel caved in, the other tumbling into the raging waves below.

The trip home was a nightmare. My dad drunk, weaving back and forth through that tunnel, and us kids screaming with terror, afraid he was going to crash into the wall, break down the barrier and drown us.

Back when I was growing up the tunnel was an old thing. Dark and stinky with fumes. Lights so low you could barely see. Tiles falling off the walls.

When traffic got backed up, I always panicked. I felt scared to death that we would be stuck inside the mile and a half long tunnel. Petrified that the walls would come crashing in drowning us like rats. I still hate that thing.

The Detroit-Windsor Tunnel is the only underwater international vehicular (automobile) tunnel in the world. Completed in 1930, the tunnel is a major border crossing and a vital socio-economic pipeline between the United States and Canada.

(*www.detroitnews.com*)

I wonder what all those fumes did to the inspectors who walked that tunnel checking for leaks and falling tiles. Do you suppose there are attorneys with ads on the television for that exposure? Probably not. I know it made me feel sick if we were in there too long.

My mother's side of the family was our support network. I only met my father's family once as they lived too far away, up north by Toronto. A long way to go for a family of six, especially a poor family with a crappy, old car.

I do remember making one trip. My dad's parents were farmers. Years of working out in the sun hardened their skin, and they almost seemed like mummies.

The memories of the journey are gone, but I can still see these two weathered, skinny, old people staring at us as we drove up to their porch.

There they sat all wrinkled and frowning, as if we looked weird to them too.

I found them frightening. I had no idea that people could look so old when I was a child.

We were raised in Detroit, Michigan, and were called Yanks by my Canadian family even though we lived just across the river. You could see downtown Windsor from the waterfront. It did not look too far away, although it was a busy waterway for ships. It ran for thirty-two miles across the state.

Back in the day, there were many goods and automobiles sent down that river on barges to other ports across the waterway. Now, manufacturing has died out and most of Detroit is a ghost town with only a few hot spots. Kid Rock and Eminem have tried different ways to revive the city. Sadly, much of it looks like a war zone.

Whenever we visited my cousins they would hoot and holler making fun of our accents. You would not think there would be much difference with the countries being so close together, but there was.

And not to let the Canucks, as they were known, off the hook, we would erupt with laughter every time they said "aye" after a sentence or when they asked a question. The Canadians are famous for that bit of lingo. They always had some sassy thing to say to us about being Yanks. We did not care, we loved them anyway.

Chapter Four

IN AN ELEPHANT herd, the oldest female is often the matriarch. My grandmother, my mother's mother, was the anchor that held the family together. Everyone loved and respected her. She never hesitated to give you a smack on the butt or shove a cookie in your mouth.

Grandmother was the person everyone turned to in their time of need. I do not know how, but she always managed to help, even if it caused her to run a little short. The family secret: she was also our resident smuggler. Oh, what a hoot.

All through my childhood, she made daily trips to and from her job as a waitress in downtown Detroit, going through that damn tunnel by bus.

When we shared our fears about the walls shattering and us drowning, everyone could count on her to say,

"If it's your time, you're going." I thought she was brave travelling through that dilapidated tunnel every day.

Most of her life, she spent waitressing to support her family. She was well-known to all the guards at both sides of the border as she travelled this route for thirty years or more. Often, they would notice when she did not make the trip and would ask after her once she reappeared. During the holidays, she gave her favorites little gift bags of homemade treats.

Every day for years and years, she went by bus back and forth through customs going through the tunnel, to get to her job.

Most things were cheaper in the states. The U.S. dollar has always been worth more than the Canadian, so grandmother would buy little things and smuggle them back in her stockings.

Back in the day, she wore these garters that were like thick rubber bands to hold up her nylon stockings. There were no panty hose back then.

I remember her coming home, whipping up her uniform skirt and pulling cans of tobacco or packs of cigarettes out of the tops of her stockings.

All around her thighs were these little smuggled items. Sometimes, she did this little penguin walk because there was so much stuff stashed under her skirt.

All the grandkids would yell, "Oh Grammy!" as she retrieved her contraband, and then we would laugh our heads off. During the war, she would carry, wear, or smuggle anything she could across the border to help someone out. It was for survival, not profit.

There are moments when bits of happy childhood memories burst from their hiding place, and, yes, there were happy ones as well as the ghosts that haunted me later.

When I reminisce, I see my grandmother in her kitchen, dressed in a short-sleeved shirt, shorts, and knee-high nylon stockings worming their way down around her ankles. She never felt fully dressed unless she had on her nylons, and it did not matter what else she was wearing. The stockings were a necessity.

Her kitchen was the hub of activity, the gathering place for everyone who visited. We would all shriek at her choice of attire as she stood there stirring a bowl of something yummy.

One day, she was slammed to the ground by a bus, while walking too close to the curb, hurrying to work. The bus mirror struck her in the back of her head as it hurried to the next stop. The weight of that big hulking machine crushed the bones in her foot.

After months of physical therapy, she admitted that she would not be able to return to her job as a waitress.

Often, the intensity of the pain was unbearable, plus her ankle would suddenly give out as the ligaments had been shredded along with the bone injuries.

Inadvertently, that forced my grandmother to retire "against her will" but it gave her a little nest egg, and we were happy to have her home when we came to visit.

Her cakes were luscious and made from the little packets that you could buy for twenty-five cents at the market. "These were cheaper than trying to do it from scratch," she'd say, and with just a few extra ingredients they were wonderful.

If you were hungry you knew you would get something good to eat at Grammy's house, and we were always hungry. Thankfully, she was always stuffing food in our faces.

Grandmother took care of everyone, even my grandfather's brothers, who had no families of their own. I have vague recollections of his brothers lounging on their couch drinking with no place to go.

Whenever anyone came from the states to visit, you had better stop at the annex and purchase a big bottle of booze and a carton of cigarettes to bring across the border. The brands were irrelevant.

My grandmother liked to have something in the house for whoever came to visit. I was so proud when I was old enough to contribute to her stockpile.

The things you could buy at the annex were tax free, so they were loads cheaper.

A pack of cigarettes in Detroit right now is about $8 depending on what brand. While in Windsor a pack cost between $12 and $15. The current exchange rate is twenty-five cents on a dollar.

For anyone planning a trip soon, you would get $1.25 of Canadian for every U.S. dollar, a definite savings.

Many an argument raged about the quality of American items versus Canadian. Of course, the river rats thought their products were much better than ours.

It did not stop them from going to Detroit and smuggling back clothes and other such contraband in the trunks of their cars.

Once, my grandmother told this story about my grandfather's brother, Leo, who bled to death right before their eyes while he was sitting on their couch tipping one back.

Leo had some type of esophageal problem, maybe cancer, which happens to many alcoholics, and something in his throat ruptured, spilling blood everywhere. As he sat there, it gurgled non-stop out of his mouth. He died before anything could be done to save him. Guess who took care of that mess? Yep, dear sweet Grammy.

My grandmother was such a strong woman. She will always be my hero. When I get bitchy, I remember how well she treated everyone, no matter their sins. Her belief was that we all make mistakes, "so just let it go."

My mother, on the other hand, was a dreamer. She worked to support us, but then she lost herself in movies and dreams of winning the Irish Sweepstakes, which had something to do with horse racing.

She and my grandmother bought tickets every year. Then they spent the rest of their time plotting how they would spend their winnings if they won. Deciding together who would and who would not get a share. Mother and daughter were very close. Mom was her first born. Those are always special.

Neither one ever did win the sweepstakes, both died penniless. But I did inherit the gene for wishful dreaming, and I have bought a lottery ticket a time or two with the hope of getting rich. After all, someone is going to win those pots, right?

As to my grandfather, I remember that he was always out hunting or fishing. We never knew when he would barge in with a fist full of rabbit ears, their little bodies dangling from his hands, or a bucket of stinky fish that he would clean at the kitchen sink.

Blood and guts were a frequent nightmare after a visit with granddad. Squeals of fright could be heard out the front door when he would offer us a tiny limb to eat, and then he would bellow with laughter, delighting in shocking whichever grandkid was visiting.

Chapter Five

I AM SURPRISED at the little snippets of my childhood I can recall. Most are full of fun times despite my parents' empty wallets.

Vacations were a non-event, but we had lots of adventures with our cousins across the river.

I remember watching my parents play cribbage. It was such a puzzle to me, fifteen two, fifteen four, and a pair is six. What kind of math were they doing? There was an "ah ha" moment when I finally understood the game and could compete with the others. Despite the poverty there are still lots of great memories before "that summer".

Some of the bright flashes are of the Halloweens we celebrated. Neighborhoods lit up like the Las Vegas strip. Noise, children running wild from house to house, treats and treasures galore. Stuffing our faces with homemade cookies and popcorn balls as fast as we could shovel them in.

Nowadays, if a rug rat gets a handmade treat, it goes right into the trash.

Many homemade treats were devoured as we zoomed up and down racing from one house to the next.

Little pieces of popcorn stuck to our cheeks and chins like that Skittles commercial as we rushed onward, afraid we would miss out on a single treat.

Razor blades and needles were a danger in the future, but not for us.

We three little ghouls went out "trick or treating" and returned exhausted, high on sugar, with our tiny pillowcases half filled with candy.

Millions of pieces of heaven spread across the front room floor. Little fingers picked out their favorites.

Strange how most of our stash vanished within a day or two. I suppose the Halloween ghosts took it back. Or maybe Mom hid it away. She had a horrible sweet tooth just like her offspring.

In prehistoric days, before the discovery of Coppertone, the tribes of the Americas were ignorant of sunblock, sunburn, or skin cancer.

They roamed free, half naked under the blazing sun in honor of their God, unaware their skin was stinging, burning, and peeling.

My parents knew nothing of these things, either. One of the few times we travelled to the beaches of Lake Erie, hours were spent frolicking in the cool crisp water.

Unprotected from the sun's burning rays, our skin cooked just like a slab of bacon. Once home, our flesh bubbled and blistered. Pain slammed into our little backs as we shivered in the cool bathwater trying to bring down the heat.

Arms and legs were burnt to the color of beet juice making it difficult to rest in our beds.

And days later, long strands of skin peeled away as the tissue died, finally giving us relief from the days of torture, as the creams and lotions were slathered on the hot spots.

Thankfully, skin cancer has not been part of our health history. Breast cancer, on the other hand was one of those cell destroying, tumor growing mutants that visited both my sister and myself later in life. That story is set in a different book.

Chapter Six

As I MENTIONED, we were Catholics and often relied on the church's charity when my father's pay checks did not come in. If it took months to finish a job, then it was months before he got his pay.

The church would give our family bags of rice, cereal, and other staples. I felt ashamed when my dad went to pick them up and bring them home, because some of the nuns had their little ways of humiliating me regarding "their" charity when they would see me in school.

At the start of the new school year, the nuns would give each family member this box of beautiful envelopes to put money into during the passing of the collection basket at mass.

The envelopes were little pouches to turn in your

pennies or such, and they were decorated with pictures of the saints or a holy day scene. The miniature paintings were so beautiful. I wish I still had a box of those lovely pictures.

Each little envelope had a tiny number on it so that, at the end of the year, they could tell which family contributed to the church. Imagine a family of six receiving six boxes, or a family of ten, getting ten boxes. How about twelve? Do I hear twelve?

Each child got her or his box. These were tough times and they expected everyone to give. Often praising those families who gave the most at the end-of-the-year assembly.

We went to mass every day before school and on Sundays. My parents would yell at us if we asked for money to put in our envelopes. "I don't have any damn money," they shouted as we trudged out the door, with them still lying in bed. I never thought that was very fair. We had to go to church, and my parents got to sleep in.

So, at church I would put the empty envelope in the collection basket hoping to fool those around me. I wanted them to think that I had given some money too. I hated the feelings that came with being poor.

I have lots of flashbacks of school plays, talent shows, presentations, and Christmas pageants. I was gregarious and talented. I was always chosen to be in the plays or talent shows. I loved showing off, at least until I no longer wanted the attention after that summer.

Many of my experiences with the nuns were very much like what you see on television. I remember getting slapped so many times I lost count over the years. I liked to talk. I liked to share my opinion. I was hit with a ruler and pinched so hard on my upper arm that it left a horrible bruise.

The little lady I would stop and visit on my way home from school called the Holy Mother to report the crazed nun who had damaged my arm. That brute eventually retired somewhere where there were no children.

I will admit that I did have my favorites. Some were kind and caring, so do not think they were all bad. They were not.

I no longer belong to any church. I have a hard time with that Cain and Abel story, and Cain going off and finding a wife. I got slapped a time or two for asking a question and then told, "you just believe." Nope not this girl: you must show me. I do believe in a higher power, but I do not believe in a God who would punish the innocent or let monsters rape and harm their children. But that is another whole book.

As I said I have memories of roaming the neighborhood chatting with folks. It was safe back then most times, although I do remember this guy flashing his penis at me while he was sitting in his car as I walked by. Disgusting pig.

I learned not to look up at people's windows, as one day I got the shock of my life when a naked man stood waving at me, shaking his whole arm back and forth like an idiot. I really think he was trying to make sure I saw him.

Another time my sister and I dressed up all pretty and went to see this neighbor boy we had a crush on. His dad came to the door with just a towel around his waist and nothing else, inviting us in to wait for Steven.

We both felt the evil radiating from inside the house as we stood outside that gaping door, while the devil invited us in. It is not just scary movies that terrify us. Sometimes it is the people we meet too.

We quickly declined and hurried home, never to see that guy or his son again.

PART II:
Shattered Trust

Chapter Seven

INCEST AND RAPE are not things we usually chose to remember. Often these memories come uninvited into our conscious minds, poking and prodding, pulling and tearing away the scab that keeps them from us.

Sometimes our memories float to the forefront of our mind like clouds in the sky. Some good, some bad. Some pretty, some ugly.

Mine have slithered out of their hiding places to assault my wellbeing at many inopportune moments, bringing forth a flood of tears.

At other times, the memories of my father's molestation burst forth like little volcanic eruptions, opening that place where they lie dormant.

I have had the scent of body powder suddenly fill my senses. Body powder was a tool my father used when he began his little bathroom games.

I do not ask to remember. I do not want to see into the past for that is where the child in me has kept things hidden for so long.

But I will confess that these memories, these real events need to be told because of the harm they did to the child, and for the way they have haunted the woman. It is time to tell my story.

I remember as a child feeling safe in my parents' love. Laughing, being silly, getting in trouble and talking my way out of everything. I would have made a great politician. And then that laughter was gone, that trust was shattered thanks to my father's sick lust for his daughters.

After that summer, I never wanted to be alone with my father. I was frightened and scared. I was afraid at night that he might come crawling into my room or call to me in the dark.

Our story started with my mother leaving. Suddenly, she was gone. I do not remember any fights. I do not remember the actual move. I just remember that one day she was gone and we little munchkins were left behind.

How does a mother leave her children? I never understood that. How could she just go off and start a new life without us? It was a year of turmoil and tragedy.

My part of the story started with my older sister leaving on vacation to stay with some cousins who came to visit. She was going to have two weeks of freedom, and I would become her replacement.

You see, there were many nights after my mother left that I would wake up alone in our bed. My sister would be gone. We shared a room and a bed. We did this for most of our childhood. My parents could not afford a big house with bedrooms for everyone, although we had twin beds for a while.

I did not ask myself too many questions about where my sister would go in the dead of night. I did not ask her. I did not even try to imagine it. I just slammed my eyelids closed and refused to acknowledge that something sinister was happening in my father's room.

You see, even though I was a child, I sensed that something was not right. Children often know when things are out of whack. They are very intuitive even if they cannot put into words what frightens them.

I remember being on our own a lot that summer. Lots of fights, pretending our tub was a swimming pool, having water fights on a hot summer day, and days of dreaming. I do not remember being upset or anxious over anything. At least not until the bathroom visits and the nights I was left alone in our bed.

So, let me start at the beginning. I was eight and my sister was close to ten. There were one and a half years between my sister and older brother, and a year and a half between my sister and myself. Remember, I said we were good Catholics. My youngest brother came five years later. I do not remember much about him. I do not even think he was there that summer.

My sister and I had no clue where our summer was headed. We trusted in the universe. We trusted our father.

Neither of us knew that under his skin was this slimy, gnarly monster, dripping spit, slithering along with an erection while he tended to his daughters.

The first time my father came into the bathroom when my sister and I were bathing we all laughed about it. He came in when we were almost done with our bath holding this pretty pink box of powder. The scent was heavenly.

Inside the box sat a soft, fluffy powder puff that felt like kitten fur, and the prettiest pink body powder. It felt like air running through my fingers. He said he wanted to show us how to put the powder on. I laughed at him saying, "Oh, Daddy, we know how to put on powder."

The room was warm and steamy, and he insisted on showing us how to powder our bodies after helping us dry off. We laughed at him thinking he was a silly head. Just like a child who thought she was safe would react. "Silly Dad."

First, he took his time drying us off because "we needed to be dry before putting on the powder."

Then, he slowly powdered me before moving onto my sister, touching us everywhere with that little powder puff. There was no fear in our hearts as we stood naked before our father. Why should we be afraid while he was putting powder here, there and every-where?

We smiled as little particles of powder scented the air and tickled our noses. And then he was gone. We smelled good and were ready for bed.

I was not frightened by his actions. I thought he was being nice giving us this lovely pink box of powder just so we could smell wonderful although when he left, so did the pink box. We thought we were so safe.

Why would any child feel fear at such a thing happening? My father had been there through many things. We did not know of evil beings in the world. We did not know that they could be disguised as our father. We did not know what kind of thing was hiding under his skin.

Then came nights when my sister would be gone from our bed. I would wake and she would not be there. I did not have a clue where she was or what was going on, but there was this weird feeling in me that something was not right, that something evil was happening.

My sister never said a word in the mornings. She never told me where she was or what was happening. Even though I was not aware of any deviant things in life, I knew that something bad was occurring.

Then came the second time my father came into the bathroom with his little pink box of powder. Right away, things felt strange. I sensed that something was totally wrong. Why was he back wanting to powder our bodies again?

The first time, I could accept his actions as a learning experience he wanted to share with us. After all, he went to all the trouble of buying us powder when we were strapped for money, but the next time felt sinister.

There was no laughter this time. There were no smiles. We just quietly waited while he did his little powdering thing and left. I remember rubbing off the powder and hurrying to our room after he left us alone. My sister and I staring at each other, not saying a word as we climbed into bed.

Could I guess now as an adult what he might have done after he left the bathroom? I will not taint your mind with what he probably was doing in his room alone after powdering his daughters little naked bodies. But it makes me sick.

The nighttime disappearances of my sister went on for a month or so, although I am not exactly sure of the time span.

In all truth, I do not even recall when the nighttime visits started. He could have been smuggling her away for some time before I became aware that she was even gone.

Then, one day our cousins showed up and offered to take my sister away on a vacation with them. We had a wonderful time together until they invited her to go back home with them to London, Ontario.

Shock slammed into me when I realized she was going to leave. I begged her not to go. I cried. I grabbed big handfuls of her shirt and pleaded for her to take me with her.

I sensed in the deepest part of my heart that if she left, whatever evil things my father was doing to her would befall me. I knew if she left, I would be her replacement. She knew it too, as she said, "Now it's your turn" as she went out the door.

If you have ever wondered how a caged animal feels, I can certainly enlighten you. My heart was filled with fear every night. Once the lights went out my heart beat like a caged animal waiting to be slaughtered. I knew

SHATTERED TRUST. A STORY OF INCEST.

SHATTERED TRUST. A STORY OF INCEST.

that it was only a matter of time before the monster came for me.

How can a child know they are endangered, but not know what that danger might entail? How can a father willingly create that kind of terror? How can an eight-year-old be so intuitive?

Chapter Eight

TEARS FLOWED DOWN my face each night as I drifted off to sleep wondering if "tonight would be the night." I would roll myself up in my blanket trying to hide my presence from the unknown, but it did not work. The beast, my father, knew where I was when he decided that it "was my turn."

I do not remember his summons. I do not remember his footsteps. I do not remember his words. I just remember him walking away, and then me following down the hallway in my little panties, heading to his room. It was summer and too hot for pajamas.

Have you ever noticed the light shining through your windows at night? It really is not dark inside the house, as the outside lights filter through the curtains giving a ghostly hue to the spaces inside.

Sometimes, the moonlight can be seen peeking through the windows, giving just a hint of brightness to the shadows. It is never truly dark, not like the darkness you get from blackout curtains, not like the darkness I so wished would hide me from the monster that beckoned.

The hallway was brushed with just a tiny bit of light as I passed by the bathroom door.

My older brother lay sleeping in his bed, not knowing I was headed into a nightmare.

In the flashback the hallway seems a long stretch of walls and floors, like a scene from an *Alice in Wonderland* movie but my father's bedroom was only three doors down, not nearly far enough to protect me.

My tiny feet left sweaty footprints behind as witnesses to my journey down that corridor. The floorboards protesting my passage.

My feet felt cold from the wood planks even though my little body was wet with sweat, as the distance vanished while I trudged forward. Breathing was difficult as his room got closer and closer. What took minutes seemed like hours.

I remember walking into my father's bedroom and standing at the side of the bed. I do not remember his words, but he must have told me to take off my panties and get into his bed, because the next flash is like the rush you get when you come out of an anesthetic.

First, I had an awareness of the dim lights, not quite dark. Shadows seemed to float around the barely lit room.

Then came the sound of crying along with the realization hitting home that it was my voice attached to the sobbing, as I noted the wetness on my face.

And the final discovery I made was that I was naked in bed with my father, and my private parts felt greasy.

I have read of cases where victims' memories have been erased as a survival mechanism by their brains. They have times where they mentally leave their bodies to avoid the horror that is ahead of them. And that's what happened to me. I have a big blank space in my memory of what my father did to me that night.

I have no memory of any fondling, penetration, or sexual act whatsoever. It was like I was not there until I heard myself crying and my brother bursting into the room to see what was going on.

The feel of grease was there in my nether regions and that has never left me. I remember seeing a jar of Vaseline on the bedspread, but I do not remember any physical contact.

Since then, I have always felt repulsed when I see a jar of Vaseline. The gunk inside that jar like a big glob of mucus. Yuck!

I did not realize there was this big empty time lapse in my memories until about six months ago when I decided to face the ghosts attached to the hauntings and write about my molestation.

I was shocked when I found emptiness where the memories lay hidden.

There is a before and an after, but that is all. What he did with that Vaseline, or how long I was in his room are pictureless memories. Dark empty spots.

Now as an adult, I struggle to imagine what might have occurred during that blank space. As I try to come up with some act that might describe what happened, it is as though the child inside of me reaches up and touches my cheek saying, "No, don't go there. Leave it," and I pull back and brush aside the images that try to appear. I realize that I do not want to "see" what my father did to his child.

Does not knowing make my experience any less traumatic? No damn way. After all the years that have passed, I still get a panicked feeling when the memories slam into me. I still feel so violated by the father that I loved and trusted. I still feel the hate I felt at his betrayal.

When I was a child, I did not realize that those kinds of things could happen. I think the emotional wound is probably the deepest. The emotions are what come back to haunt me. The feeling of panic, of fear, of being afraid of my father. I do not remember all the details of the abuse, so that is probably the reason that the emotions are so strong.

The trauma that my father inflicted on me sears me. The shock that he would do something like that, whatever that was, sickens me. For him to come into the bathroom like a loving parent, and then unleash this creature to assault us. What a despicable demon was hidden beneath his smile.

Every single time I was assaulted with the memories of that summer there was that emptiness. I never questioned it as the flashes burnt holes in my heart.

I would quickly brush away the before and after pictures that would burst into my mind for brief seconds, never analyzing what I was seeing. At least not until I decided to write it all down, and then I realized that I did not know what actually happened that summer.

At the first realization of those lost memories, I froze as I tried to bring the images forward and found that the child had locked those memories away, never to be retrieved by the child or the adult.

I now see that I will never know exactly what evil deeds my father did that night, and part of me is extremely glad that the memories have been forever hidden away.

Chapter Nine

MY BROTHER WAS my shining knight that evening when he burst into the room asking, "What's going on in here?"

Normally, we did not get along. I was just someone to push around, but I was his someone, and he did not want my father hurting me. Maybe he already knew of my sister's nighttime visits to my father's room.

When he came into that bedroom demanding to know what the heck was happening, he turned into my new best friend, at least in that moment, years later not so much.

I remember my father telling him to come in and sit down as if nothing evil had just happened as he told us his (bullshit) story. He told us he was dying of cancer, the bastard. He said he had been to New York for treatment although we had no memories of him ever being gone. He lied and said there was nothing that could be done for him. He was going to die.

Oh, what a monster, he was weaving his tale of death to escape the crimes he had committed on his daughters. What an evil creature to lie to us and make us feel bad for him after he did whatever it was that he did to me.

We were just children. We cried. We felt terrible that he was going to die. He used our emotions against us, and then sent us back to our rooms.

After my brother left and as I was leaving, my father told me he would buy me a big bottle of soda, whatever brand I wanted, and that he would pick it up tomorrow on his way home from work. He advised me not to tell anyone about his cancer, or what had happened that night. He said he did not want anyone to know he was "dying." I waited years and years for that monster to die.

I do not remember anything after I left my father's room. I do not remember if I put my panties back on or carried them down the hall or if I wiped myself off. I do not remember getting in bed or going to sleep.

But I do remember waiting all the next day for my father to come home with my big liter of cream soda. As if that could make everything alright. You see soda pop was a rarity in our house. It was a treat. Something we almost never were given.

Well, the beast came home empty-handed tossing aside his promise to me as if nothing had even happened the night before. I felt betrayed. I felt ashamed that I foolishly waited for his offering of forgiveness when none was going to be offered.

I felt betrayed when he fussed at me when I asked for my soda pop. I felt raped all over again—if that is what occurred the night before—as he sat in his chair and drank a beer.

When my sister came back, I never said a word to her about what had happened. I did not remember most of it anyway, just the bits and pieces I shared with you.

I do remember hating her as she came home all smiles, having had a wonderful time away. I knew that she knew our father had had his go at me. I was angry for years with her as I felt that she had abandoned me to him.

He never mentioned what he did to me, what he did to my sister. I can honestly say I do not remember if my sister's nighttime visits continued or how long it was before my mother came home. I just know that when my mother returned after a year, my father acted like a saint instead of the demon he was.

I wish that my sister and I would have talked about what happened. Shared our feelings. We never have, but I hope the next time we are together we will be able to talk about what our father did to us. We were children, raped by a parent we trusted. I want to try to get her to talk, to share, to cry, and to let out the hate we both must feel toward our father because those feelings have never gone away for me.

I want to say to all those rapists out there, those pedophiles, those incestuous bastards who see their children as sex objects: I hope you rot in hell.

Whatever crime you committed on the child you were entrusted to watch over and protect, you have left a dark mark on their soul forever; it has ruined a part of them. Even if they hid it away, never to speak of it, buried it deep in a dark place, it still crushes them every time the memories escape.

The damage committed to that tiny child can never be completely undone. The memories will haunt them for all time. The fear they must have felt at your hands is now a piece of their DNA.

PART III:
Revelation

Chapter Ten

So WHAT HAPPENS next in this story of incest? This terrible revelation of a childhood that was shattered, because that little child was never the same afterwards. Well, the next part is how and when the story came out, for surely it did one Christmas night.

I first want to say that many children never reveal their trauma to their family. They never find the courage to talk about it, to disclose the horror that has occurred. Many adults hide from their suspicions of rape or incest, too frightened to even contemplate such an act.

Most adults just want to hide from the thought of such a thing ever happening. Most do not want to talk about the possibility or even the probability of such a horrible thing being inflicted on their child.

They often do not give that child the chance to tell their story when the abuse is exposed. That is what happened to me. I never got to tell my story after my brother revealed our darkest secret. It stayed hidden all my life. Not once have I revealed this story of abuse to anyone.

My sister returned from her vacation all smug and happy. I hated her in that moment. We never talked about the time she was gone on her little vacation. The fact that I had indeed become her replacement.

Now that I am older, I can see from her perspective. It was probably such a great relief for her. She no doubt felt she was escaping a prison, a nightmare.

I really do not know her feelings. I can only imagine. But I do forgive her for leaving me as I surely would have done the same thing—if someone would have offered me an escape route, as I walked down that dark hallway.

I have no memories of when exactly my mother returned home. I do remember my father taking us to see her in the city. She had moved away to a cute little apartment in downtown Detroit. She was independent of him and her children. Who cared what happened to us!

I remember seeing her little place, it was so cute, so tidy, and she looked so happy. We all stood there in the doorway like the beggars we were. I do not even recall going in the apartment, just standing there "waiting".

I suppose they must have talked. It is all a blur, and then one day she was back. Back among her family. I often wondered if she missed her cute little apartment, her independence. I can understand now how she must have longed for a life of her own. Married at age seventeen, and then bang three children under six. Number four, five years later.

What a hell it must have been for her. I am sorry she never had the life she desired. I remember hearing whispers between her and my grandmother when they did not realize I was there.

It was her chance to get away, and she missed it. I often wondered if she knew the creature that resided under my father's skin. If he slobbered over her in the bathroom as he powdered her body. Maybe that is why she left. I will never know.

Chapter Eleven

I HAVE NO more memories of my sister's absence in the dead of night after she returned from her vacation. I am sure I went to bed and closed my mind to everything around me, too frightened to pay attention.

I do not remember how long it was before my mother returned home. I only know that she was gone for a year.

Life just went on after she came back. I cannot say they were happy. I cannot say they were not. We were all just back together.

My sister and I never spoke to anyone about what happened while my mother was living the good life. My brother and I never spoke about it either. It was the elephant in the room that none of us would acknowledge. We were simply happy that Mom had returned, and I for one did not want to spoil it and have her leave us again, so the stories of that summer got buried away.

There was one terrible time when we had visitors. I do not know who these visitors were, friends or family, but they were sleeping over. My sister and I were told our dad would sleep with us as there were no extra bedrooms. My mother declared that the visitors would have their room, and she would sleep on the couch when she came home from work.

All I can say is that, son of a bitch, I was scared! I could not believe that my mother was going to put our father in our room. I know that she did not have a clue about what he had done to us, but I freaked out. I cried, begged her to let him sleep on the couch, let me sleep on the couch.

I told her our bed was too small and I made up every kind of story I could to try and keep myself safe. I was horrified that he might try something again if he got me alone. Eventually, I was sent off to bed early just to get me out of her hair.

I have memories of avoiding any contact with my

dad after that summer. We never touched again. I kept my distance and avoided him whenever I could. I tried to never be alone in the same room with him.

Can you image this little child rushing out of the room or hurrying to bed early just so she could hide away, because she was afraid of her father? He did that to me!

Even after my mother returned home, I spent years trembling in my bed afraid I would hear his footsteps, afraid of hearing his voice late at night calling me. Every creak of the floor, every groan of the wind outside sent me spiraling into a place filled with fear.

It was awful that night as I lay crying. My face soaked and my pillow drenched. I had sweated through my pajamas when I rolled myself up in my blanket like a burrito, in the hopes that my father could not get to me when he came into our room.

All I can say is I was terrified. I was so petrified that he would do something to me if he thought no one was watching.

When my sister came into the room to go to bed, she lost all patience with my crying and sobbing, shoving me back against the wall with her on the outside of the bed just to shut me up. She was not afraid of him. At least that is how she acted.

I remember being squashed against the wall with the blanket all tangled around me waiting and waiting to hear his footsteps. I could not go to sleep. Each sound sent a wave of terror rushing through my body, and a rainstorm of tears down my face.

When he finally showed up, he was so drunk he just dropped onto the bed and passed out. After listening to his spastic snores for what seemed like hours, I was finally able to let go of my fear and fall asleep. And I was very relieved to find him gone when I woke up.

What a nightmare for that little girl. How could a father knowingly create such fear in his little daughter's heart? Did he really think he would not, with his abuse? Did he have any thoughts about the damage he had done? I am sure he did not. I am sure he did not care! He never displayed any remorse before or after my mother returned home.

Chapter Twelve

THERE IS NO easy way to reveal such a dramatic tale of incest, especially for this family. My brother came home drunk and spit out the story during my mother's Christmas party. None of us had ever talked about it. Neither my sister nor I whispered a word to anyone. We just went on with life after my mother returned, but there was this great distance between us. I felt very alone for quite some time. I trusted no one.

We settled into a routine as a family. Nothing spectacular happening. Just everyday stuff, except that my mother was starting to feel "happy" with life and decided to host a Christmas party for our family, and the relatives across the river.

The Canadians had never come to celebrate with us at our house, we always congregated at my grandmother's during the holidays. That Christmas was a first for all of us.

It took years for our families to build a little security. Now that my parents were back together, and work seemed to be good, my mother wanted to share it with her clan.

It was a fabulous Christmas party. Mom had prepared lots of wonderful dishes as she was a hell of a cook. There were piles of delectable things everywhere, endless bottles of alcohol, mountains of gifts, and lots of noise and chaos. Loud voices, laughter, music, and kids screaming as they loaded up on the sugary treats filled every room.

Our house was brimming with laughter and happiness like never before. You could feel it in the air. The weather was glorious, and it felt wonderful having the whole family at our house. I was proud of my mother, and you could tell by her swagger that she was proud too.

Of course, you know when there is that much happiness, and that much booze, something has got to give eventually. There are always fights and tears when you get a bunch of alcoholics together, and my relatives were the kings and queens of alcoholics. Many get-togethers ended with fights and tears, people leaving angry and children afraid of the outcome once they got home.

Suddenly through the noise and chaos we could hear my father and brother shouting at each other. Loud intangible words of anger. My brother was intoxicated, so he felt brave in his arrogance. Being only fourteen or so, he decided for some reason that now was the time to attack my father for what he had done in the past, celebration be damned.

Out of the blue my brother yelled at my father, "You have no right getting pissed at me, you're the bastard who was molesting his own daughters."

All sound fell through the floorboards as my brother's last words echoed around the room. No one missed the exchange, no one missed what had been tossed out between father and son.

Abruptly everyone froze, staring at each other at the secret that had been revealed. It was like a scene in a movie where they freeze the action. For the briefest moment no one moved or said a word, and then all hell broke loose.

It felt like an earthquake; you could feel the floors vibrating as the herd trampled each other trying to escape. The doors swinging on their hinges as everyone fled, sure of the fury to be unleashed.

My mother started screaming and telling people to leave. Relatives were scrambling to grab their stuff and escape. My grandmother was trying to calm my mother. My mother was yelling and attacking my father as he rushed out the door. My brother ran out the door like a little coward, and my sister and I rushed to our bedroom to hide from everyone.

It was a nightmare to say the least. The one time my mother tried to have a great night and it was shattered. Shattered like my trust in my father years ago.

The worst part, the most horrible part of the whole thing, was when my mother came rushing into our room and started slapping my sister hard across the face calling her names. "Whore! Slut!" she screamed. Using both hands, she slapped one check and then the next.

My sister never cried as she was being pummeled.

She just stared at our mother as she was assaulting her, while I hid under the covers, not wanting my mother to turn her anger on me.

I have always felt horrible over my cowardice. I felt I should have defended my sister. I should have told my mother that it was both of us he molested, but instead I just hid, not wanting to be a recipient of the violence she was inflicting on my sister. For that I am a traitor.

You might ask: why did my mother direct her anger at my sister? How was my sister responsible for my father's depravity? Why do people blame the victim, for surely, they do! And that is a crime itself, to blame the victim, what stupidity!

How could my sister or me protect ourselves when we had no idea what evil plans my father had in store for us?

If we wanted to blame someone—if we needed to blame someone other than my father—then we could have blamed my mother for leaving us behind with that monster.

Surely, she knew what kind of creature he was. If I were going to blame someone it would be her, not my sister, not me, not the victims.

I do not know if my mother and sister ever talked, but I really hope they did before she died, as my mother needed to apologize for that night. My sister and I were innocent victims of a parent's sick lust. We were not to blame for anything.

It was the Christmas that changed all our lives forever. My dad left that night followed by a flurry of obscenities. I do not remember him ever coming back to collect his belongings or any other contact with him. It was ten years before I saw him again.

It broke up our family which was okay with me. I never wanted to see him again, but it did not provide the relief from what my father did to us, as one might hope.

I do not know what story was told by my brother, or to whom, but no one sat us down to talk. No one asked us what happened. No one ever allowed me to share my feelings about that summer. It was shoved under the rug, so to speak, never discussed by any family member.

The shame was heavy on my shoulders and I did not visit my Canadian family for some time, unable to bear their pitiful looks or questioning eyes. I felt tainted and ashamed. I felt like a creature in a zoo when we would go to visit.

Everyone would get quiet as we entered the room. It took years for me to bury the shame I felt so I could face them again and feel relaxed enough to laugh. Here lies one of the many ways my father destroyed our family.

PART IV:
Hauntings

Chapter Thirteen

HAUNTINGS IS A good description of what has been happening to me throughout my life. I have been haunted by the memories of that summer. Three tiny episodes that damaged a small part of me. In my memory the childhood before "that summer" was good. Everyone had hard times unless you came from a wealthy family. It was the fifties, only a decade since the war. So childhood was a struggle off and on for everyone as they tried to settle and get established.

But then that summer happened, and the fear and memories were embedded into my being. The memories became ghosts of a summer past when my father molested my sister and me. That time when he shattered our trust.

I will bear that throughout my life, these memories

that erupt like little volcanic bursts. For no reason I am jutted back in time to that hallway or to our empty bed with my sister gone missing.

I am a ghost standing in my father's room by his bed. I am a ghost in his bed with greasy private parts. I am haunted by the crying of that child, knowing it is me, and I am haunted by the fear of what just happened to that child, haunted by the fear she felt.

Over and over through my lifetime these memories have wormed their way out of their hiding place to remind me of that wounded little girl. I hope by the telling of my story it will help others to tell their stories and release their ghosts as well.

Long ago, I believed that what my father did to me was a lone wolf event. That real people, real fathers did not do those kinds of things to their children. I thought it was just my father who was sick, no one else was that evil.

But the truth is different. If you really want to feel disgusted Google the statistics of the children who are molested or raped by a family member or friend. Look at those who are attacked and molested by a stranger.

Rape and incest are so prevalent that it can only cause a deep sadness within our hearts that humanity has taken such a sick turn.

You would be horrified to learn the number of children who are captured and enslaved for sex. You can Google loads of statistics regarding the number of girls and women who have been forced to turn to prostitution after they were made addicts by their perpetrators. The numbers are staggering. The day-to-day numbers of crimes against children are unbelievable.

A large percentage of these crimes are committed by men, but the statistics also reveal that there is a small percentage of women who get off on torture, seeing children raped, and raping children. But the huge number, the huge, huge number of perverts and pedophiles are men. Many of them buying girls and children from other countries to enslave them, until they deem them trash and throw them away.

Others steal them from their mothers, their homelands, raping them for years until they are too mature for their taste, and then they are cast aside or passed on to another. These victims are left ruined and destroyed.

Psychologically traumatized for the rest of their lives.

Even in our dear United States of America there is child slavery, child prostitution, and child pornography. Kidnappings and transportation across state lines, cross boundaries and borders happen all the time.

Some say the United States is one of the biggest gluts of childhood prostitution. And the most heartbreaking part of all of this is that most people close their eyes to what is going on. No one wants to believe that such evil exists, but it does.

No one wants to point a finger. What a disgusting thing to even imagine or hold true. Yet what of these children, these young boys and girls, these girls who have had their youth and lives stolen from them? They will never be innocent or carefree again. They will never be free from the hauntings.

Who is going to come out and save them? We need to shout from the rooftops the names of these sick bastards who are raping our children.

We need to reveal those who prey on the weaker ones. You know the story of Jeffrey Epstein and all his big friends, including a president and a prince, who used teen girls for their pleasure. Taking them up in planes to party where the world could not see what was happening.

Princes, and other wealthy clients of this monster hiding on a private island to use and abuse these young girls. Most have never been tried or punished. The records hidden away.

The only one sent to jail other than Epstein (who supposedly committed suicide while in a safe prison) has been the madame who was instrumental in acquiring these young girls. The actual perpetrators of these crimes are free to walk among us without any punishment or retribution paid by them.

How sick is the world where a man would rape his children? How sick is humanity when young girls and boys are stolen from their homes and used as sex slaves until they are worthless, to be thrown away like pieces of garbage. We must do something as a society. We must not close our eyes to it. We must not turn our heads away. We must call out the abusers. We must let the world know.

Keeping things quiet will never help the victims feel

better. Nothing can be as painful as the experiences. No words voiced can be more traumatic than the sexual abuse.

I was never given the chance to talk about my experience. My family looked the other way. They did not ask me how I was doing, or what really happened. They never asked about me walking down that dark hallway in my little panties having no clue what was before me.

I knew not what sick thoughts were in my father's head. I went because there was still a little trust there. I could not fathom what he would do, what he would say. And that is what these sick animals rely on. That you cannot guess what they have planned.

The statistics reveal only an inkling, an exceedingly small inkling of the rapes and molestations that are committed daily. I pray that this revelation will encourage you to fight against these crimes with pen and paper, with phone calls to the police, of turning in family members or friends who perpetrate these horrendous crimes on the innocent.

Let them face charges. Let the children speak. The revealing of the story will be so much less painful than the damage done to their little bodies and minds. It will give them the chance to be believed, to be loved, to be nurtured, to be supported in their pain while they watch these bastards get punished. It is not more painful to tell than it is to live.

We must stop the beasts from hunting and devouring our young. We must punish those who have stolen the innocence of so many. We must help those wounded souls find some peace in their otherwise horrendous lives.

I do not think you want to hear my true feelings, but I will tell you anyway. I believe in castration; I believe in lobotomies. I believe those who have raped and maimed our young must be imprisoned like the animals they are for the rest of their natural lives. Some would say that is not humane. I say these are not humans.

No human would inflict any kind of humiliating sexual act against a child—hell, against anyone. Only a monster could do these kinds of things. Only a gargoyle would enjoy the torture of another. Only a demon could do such horrendous acts. These are not humans. They are not even subhuman. Do not feel sorry for them. Do not pray for them. Pray for their victims.

I know that we have all heard the statistics that many of these vile humans have been victims of abuse themselves, as children. I am so sorry for their experiences, but it does not excuse the harm they have inflicted on others.

Their trauma should not allow their offenses to go unpunished. Just like an alcoholic usually has a history of parental alcoholism, many of these perpetrators have been victims as well at the hands of some sick person.

Ask a victim if that makes the crime against them excusable, unpunishable, and you will hear a resounding, "NO."

I have never molested anyone. I have never felt the need to hurt another. I am disgusted to think that someone would use their pain to cause pain to an innocent child.

How could their rational mind not tell them that what they are doing is so vile, so wicked, and evil?

How can they hear the cry of their victims and not feel horrified at the deeds they have done? How can anyone expect another to "just let it go" when it will haunt them for the rest of their lives?

Chapter Fourteen

IF THERE WAS one thing I would recommend to victims of incest and rape, it would be to get your story out into the open. Talk about it. Share it with someone. It is not as if it is going to suddenly heal you or make it go away—it is not. It is more about affirming that it happened to you. The more you talk about it, say it out loud, the more you acknowledge that a **crime** has been committed against you, the more you affirm yourself.

And the more you share your story the better you will feel because keeping it hidden and quiet will only cause the wound from your trauma to go deeper and do more damage.

Keeping things quiet has not helped me. It has always been there, erupting at the oddest moment. Coming to the forefront of my thoughts when that was not even the topic. Suddenly, it was like a little creature sitting on my shoulder whispering, "Remember that summer, remember it?"

For me I do not believe anything is going to make the memories go away, make it okay, and I do not think it should be **okay**. I think we should be upset and angry that our trust was shattered by someone we thought would protect us, love us, and keep us safe. The very thought that someone we loved could violate us is incomprehensible.

Talking about it, speaking it out loud, helps shrink that inner demon, shrink that place inside that holds it, that place that feels rancid, that place where the memories hide out.

I was violated. I do not remember all the details, but when I have tried to remember I feel sick inside. I panic, my mind withdraws from the releasing of the details. The loss of my memory does not lessen my trauma.

Whether you are molested once, or many times, each time matters. Each time is an offense against that little child, it is a **crime**. Each instance of abuse will burn a hole in their tiny heart. It will create demons for them to fight throughout their lives.

What acts against a child would you deem a molestation, a crime? A father having his child sit on his lap while he becomes sexually excited? Fondling, touching, peeking at their nakedness when the child is unaware? Forcing the child to allow them to perform sexual acts on their person or forcing the child to perform sexual acts on them?

When my father came into that bathroom to play his powder puff games, he was molesting my sister and myself. Unbeknownst to us he was getting pleasure out of seeing and touching our little naked bodies. He was planning his next move. In my nightmares I see him as this slimy creature with his tongue flapping out of his mouth, spit falling on the floor, and this gaping hole of a mouth smiling with glee.

My abuse happened the summer after my mother moved out. Why she left I do not know. I do not want to contemplate all that he might have done under the guise of a loving father while living together as a family, as that is too sick, too revolting to imagine. But I must ask myself now that I know he was a deviant, a pedophile: what other acts upon our little bodies did he perform that were for sexual gratification and not just the love of a parent?

This has haunted me for sixty-two years. It's been sixty-two years since it happened, and I can still be brought to tears. My brain protected me from all that happened back then. I do not remember ALL the details. Just bits and pieces. But those bits and pieces have the power to hurt me, to make me sad, and make me so angry.

Do you not think a child should feel fear when their own father comes into the bathroom to powder their naked bodies and gawk at them for his own sick pleasure? Do you not think a child should be sickened and frightened by a parent who wants to grease their private parts and fondle them, if that is what happened? Do you not think a child should be traumatized by a father who greased their private parts and tried to penetrate them, if that is what he did? Do you not think he should rot in hell because I do!

I do not know what he did, but I feel terrified when the thoughts come uninvited to the forefront of my memories. Ghosts that try to escape and haunt me.

The fact that I do not remember all the things my father did to me, did not lessen my fear, my panic when I was a child. I think the not knowing made it worse because when I tried to remember it was unbearable.

I feel sick and broken hearted because the father that I always loved chose to abuse me for his own depravity instead of keeping me safe from such monstrous acts.

People hear the topic and want to know the gory details, but I cannot tell them to you. I only remember the before and the end. The middle, the actual event, is a big black empty hole.

What happened after I stepped into that room is gone forever, but the fear that was planted that day has never gone away. All I have left is a sick feeling inside, like a big heavy wet lump of clay laying in the middle of my gut. Sadly, for me, all the players in this sick drama are gone. I will never be able to ask my questions or have answers to the "why of it."

So, I want to encourage others to talk about what has happened to them. Say it out loud to people.

Acknowledge it. It happened; it is real. It will affect your whole life, just like it did mine.

Tell yourself that you were a victim of an extremely sick monster, and that you had nothing to do with it. It may help kill the demon inside.

I have read of cases where the child eventually became a willing participate in the pervert's sick games.

I want to tell these victims that we are all sexual beings. Searching for sexual gratification throughout our lives. Because the person who molested you knew how to groom you to enjoy the pleasure of that sexual act, does not mean that it was not a crime against you. For surely it was. We can feel sexual pleasure and still be repulsed by our reactions.

Letting others know what happened may help with the sorrow you feel. It may help with the heartbreak of it. To be able to avoid feeling like you need to hide the awful things done to you may help put the ghost to rest.

No one gave me the chance to speak. No one asked me how I was violated. No one asked what my father did. No one talked about it. We just went on like nothing happened, even though inside I felt this boiling mass of lava, gurgling and churning, waiting to erupt.

I remember once my grandmother tried to talk me into going and seeing my father. I was a teenager by then, I do not remember what age, but she tried to get me to go visit him, telling me that he was getting old, and that he wanted to see me.

Her request slammed into my chest like a brick. I could not believe she would suggest such a thing. I looked at her like she was crazy. It is the only time in my life when my grandmother really disappointed me.

She made me feel terrible when she asked for me to put aside my feelings, even though she did not know how awful I felt because we never talked about the molestation of my sister and me.

She, too, never asked, and never let me talk about what he did. She was there when the story was thrown out in the middle of my mother's Christmas party, but she never questioned us afterwards.

I was so disgusted that she would take his side and not feel horrified, angry, and want to murder him as I did for the things he did to my sister and me.

What a huge disappointment! I wanted to shout the

words out loud to her. I wanted to tell her right there and then what he did, and I was a heartbeat away from it when she turned and walked away. I think she could tell by the look on my face that she was awfully close to hearing things that she really did not want to hear.

How can people expect the victim of incest to let it go when they do not even know the horrible story? How could she ask me to feel sorry for him when she did not have a clue that he greased my lower parts with Vaseline so he could do whatever it was he had tried to do.

How can anyone ever understand your pain if they do not hear the details of the rape, of the molestation? If they do not listen to what you had to endure at the hand of someone you trusted and loved. How can they know how you were violated if they do not let you speak the words?

Chapter Fifteen

MY GRANDMOTHER SHOULD have been telling my father to fall on his knees and beg for my forgiveness. She should have attacked him like an angry lioness for hurting her cub. She should have come to my defense, not ask me to put aside my feelings.

And he should have begged for my forgiveness. He should have talked to me. He should have answered my questions of, "Why did you do that Daddy, why?"

I wanted to ask my grandmother how he could look at that skinny little child (I can see her in my mind's eye, just a little tiny thing), how he could look at her and lust. How is it possible, what twisted distorted part of his brain said it was okay?

If we can talk about it, we can release a little bit of the sorrow. If we can tell our stories over and over it will help us with the pain of it. It will help us with the shame, because we do feel shame over the acts of our fathers.

It was not my fault. I was not provocative or enticing. I never wanted it to happen. I was barely eight years old, but I felt so much shame for what was done to me. I felt so ashamed that someone would find out what kind of monster lived under the guise of my father.

As I said numerous times, I was never given the opportunity to talk about the incest. No one spoke about it, but one time when I was about twelve or thirteen, my mother and I were driving in a car somewhere, and my father's name came up. I am not sure of the conversation, but it had a hint of the past, and I looked her in the eye waiting to hear what she would say. I felt that sudden sense of panic that came from remembering. My breath caught in my throat.

I think she said something about being sorry for hitting my sister or something to that affect, and I looked at her and said, "Me, too, Mom, me too"…meaning he had molested me as well. After all those years I still could not speak the words out loud.

Her eyes blinked like she had just been slapped, then she looked away as she lightly nodded her head like she knew, but our conversation never went any further, it ended right there!

She turned away from me and continued driving, and I turned and looked out my window, neither of us ever mentioning the abuse again.

Adults that are not twisted in the ways of a pervert or pedophile are horrified. They are disgusted. They are angered. They feel so helpless, and they panic at the thought of that kind of abuse. I understand that reaction, but the sad part of this is that they shut out the child in their time of need.

The adults are so horrified at what has been done that they do not give the child a chance to cry in their arms over the trauma they have experienced.

They do not give them the chance to be loved, to be reassured that someone will keep them safe from here on in. I needed that, I never got it.

As a little child I had to suffer alone. I had no one to assure me that I was safe. I spent years afraid at night that the monster would return. I do not think I had a good night's sleep until after my father moved out that Christmas.

Every night, I listened to the squeaks of the floorboards as they settled into place imagining it was my father.

I strained to hear the footsteps I believed were in the hallway heading my way, fearing my father was sneaking toward our room to start what he had done in the past again.

I would toss and turn until I was utterly exhausted, and then, only then could sleep finally overtake my little body.

One night, I could hear my father roaming around in the kitchen. My bladder screaming at me to get out of bed. The fear keeping me glued to the mattress until I felt the wetness sliding from between my legs. I was not able to wait for the monster to return to his lair, and shamefully wet the bed.

One of the worst things is when a person says they want to help a child, but they do not want to hear about the acts themselves. They do not allow them to say the words out loud.

I do not even know what I would have said about what happened. I was sickened, sad, and frightened. I had no support person to help me through those events. Not my mother, not my sister, nor my brother. No one seemed to care what happened to us. It was as if it did not matter what evil things my father inflicted on my sister and me. Life just went on.

Any person who professes the desire to help a victim must swallow their own revulsion at the stories and allow the victims to express their pain. These victims need to get the whole story out.

Do you think your pain of knowing is going to be worse than their pain of experiencing the rape, the incest? Hell no! If you do not let them get it out it scabs over going deeper inside, and then it oozes with the truth when they least expect it.

It is like a giant iceberg of pain with the biggest part hidden under the skin, far bigger than that on the surface. It's much larger than you can imagine until the explosion occurs from the pain they have suppressed.

As hard as it will be for a parent or family member to hear the things that were done to a child, it is a thousand times harder on that child to remember and not be able to tell. They need to share the story, the trauma. They need to express their horror at what was done to them. They need to know they are not at fault, that it was a sick person who did those things to them. Only someone who loves that child can give them back the sense of safety they so desperately need.

It is going to be painful for everyone when the story is revealed, but it is so important to that child to share it. Left untold the pain will go deeper and deeper like the crust of a wound. That crust will keep getting bigger until eventually it ruptures, causing mass destruction to that child, and all those around them—just like the destruction that occurred when my brother spit out our story during my mother's Christmas celebration.

Chapter Sixteen

IN THE WHOLE scheme of things, all the traumatic acts that I have read in other people's stories led me to think, "Boy, my story is almost nothing." But what I have come to accept, and what I want to emphasize to people and other victims is that it is not a competition for whose trauma is the worst.

It is not a contest of whose story is the most disgusting! Or whose story went on the longest, because everyone's story reveals a **crime** against another human being.

Everyone's story should bring about a feeling of anger over the harm brought to another person. Everyone's story is a shame on humanity.

The fact is, whatever the act of incest, it leaves that child scarred for the rest of their life. This thing that has happened has left a wound in their heart. It shattered their trust and filled them with fear of a family member, father, or friend forever.

It does not matter the crime. It was a crime. My story is about how my father wounded my soul. How he crushed and destroyed the love I felt for him. How he gouged out a part of my heart.

Anytime a parent or another person violates a child it is a horrendous act against their person, and it is going to leave a deep emotional wound in their heart.

So, it is not a contest of whose story is the worst, because any form of incest or rape is traumatic for that victim. The atrocious deeds done will create nightmares and hauntings for years, maybe a lifetime like mine.

I want to tell all the victims out there: "Do not try to belittle your trauma. Do not push it aside. Do not mislabel it. It was an abomination against your innocence."

I believe I did that a lot. I told myself that I only had three "tiny" episodes compared to so many others who were violently brutalized or wounded.

I would ask myself: "How can I compare my experiences to theirs? How can I feel badly about what happened to me?" After reading the horrible acts other victims had to endure, I thought, "Shit, my trauma was nothing."

I think that because there is an empty hole in my memory. A big gaping abyss of nothingness (as I have no memory of what else happened after I walked into that room). I felt that it did not count in relation to the trauma of other stories I have read.

When I close my eyes and stand at the edge of that abyss, I cannot see what he did while applying grease to my private parts. I cannot see what happened. I really do not know. But I do not think it matters. The child inside of me knows, and she chose to bury it away.

Once upon a time, I believed that I lived in a safe world. I did not realize that I lived with a monster who was plotting to take away my innocence. I could not see the sinister thoughts lurking in my father's mind when he looked at me. I thought he loved me. I thought he would keep me safe. I did not see that he was preparing to shatter my trust. To assault my innocence.

Chapter Seventeen

THERE ARE SO many questions haunting my mind about that summer. Was my father lurking in the shadows when I was unaware? Was he planning what he was going to do to my sister and me days or weeks ahead? Was he figuring out how he would get one of us into his bed? What were his thoughts? Was he always filled with lust for his daughters, my father? Was it always there?

You know this could be just a book of questions. How could he? Why would he? Why didn't I tell on him? Why didn't I confront him? What evil lurked inside of him? Why did he do it? How could he go through with molesting us, possibly raping us?

There are a lot of how questions in my mind. How could you look at this little skinny girl, your child, and feel lust? There was not a sexual thing about his little daughter. How could my father look at this scrawny little child and plan to molest her? For plan it he did, starting with the powder.

The ever-present fact is that I will never know the answer to my questions. I will never know how he could look upon us and be sexually aroused. How he could plan this in his mind for days. It was not like he suddenly thought he would buy a box of powder for us. He must have planned it. He must have picked out the perfect little box. Something pretty! Something that smelled just right!

He must have thought about how he would come into the bathroom while we were taking a bath and trick us into letting him fondle us with that powder puff. What a twisted monstrosity my father turned out to be.

I contemplated checking the statistics of children who have been raped or molested by a parent or family member, but you can never trust the numbers the statisticians end up with. Most cases go unreported to counting houses or law enforcement.

Many victims are never freed from their bondage: many are never given the chance to tell their stories.

Many are left too wounded to talk about the horrors they had to endure.

If you have watched the news or scanned Yahoo lately you have seen the most recent stories of politicians, coaches, priests, and other childhood mentors who have victimized their little wards.

People that others trusted with their children's lives, abusing that trust and that child. Daycare workers who have molested the children in their care for years. How can those numbers not haunt many a person?

One site I found reported that **every nine minutes, a child is a victim of sexual abuse by someone they know.**

So, **every nine minutes a child is being molested somewhere.**

Every nine minutes a child is being molested somewhere in this country.

Every nine minutes a child somewhere in this country is being molested by someone they love.

That should catch your breath; it should stop your heart. I know it makes a lot of people recoil, shy away from this topic because it is too terrible. Picture how it is for those who are forced to experience it!

Every nine minutes a child is molested in this country, often by someone they trusted.

When I decided to write my story, I was driven by the memories that never went away. The flashes that came like little firecrackers popping into my brain at odd times to remind me.

The memories bursting into my awareness interrupting whatever thoughts were just floating around in my head. No rhyme or reason. The ghosts escaping at the oddest times. And then I remember that summer. I still feel the emotional pain of those episodes when my father molested me, for that is what he surely did.

I want to shout out loud to anyone who is comparing their trauma to others and trying to downplay the horror of it: Do not do that! Every touch, every act that was forced upon you is just as horrible as anyone else's. It is something that should never happen to any child, by anyone. These things are a crime against you. You are the victim.

The big message I want to send out into the world is

that even the small things are dreadful for a child.

I want to get it out to others like me who might think that their sexual abuse "wasn't so bad": that everything, every deviant thing that is done to us, every sick instant of abuse maims us, leaves a mark on our soul even if it is one thing or two things or twenty or thirty.

To think that human beings can inflict such horrid things on children. To be faced with the reality of it. To see or hear about the monstrous things that they do is just, there is not a good enough word in the English language to describe my revulsion.

The word horrifying is not enough, the word disgusting is not enough. There is no word good enough to describe the impact of that kind of treatment by a father, by an uncle, or family friend.

The deed done by someone who this child loved and trusted is unthinkable. That a child is forced to see what awful things could happen in their world is atrocious.

And I am only talking about incest right now. I am not even talking about the millions of children being raped or molested by strangers. I am not talking about the millions sold into bondage, abducted and hidden away for some person's sick pleasure.

I am not talking about the millions of lives stolen, although I should, although we should. Those are crimes so vile, so deviant, so wicked that none of us should be able to sleep in our beds at night.

None of us should be able to rest without doing or saying something to bring an end to these crimes against humanity, against our very own children.

One of the many reasons behind revealing my story is to talk about my trauma. For me, the story just needed to come out.

I have never shared my trauma before writing this book, and I believe that is why it forever haunts my thoughts. Your story needs to come out too, you need to share it with somebody, somehow, in some form. You need to release the demon that is smothering you, that is creeping up on your shoulder when you least expect it, to whisper in your ear, "Hey remember this, remember that"… leaving you feeling shattered all over again.

Those memories are scars that are not going to go away, you will carry those battle wounds forever. Those are memories that will always haunt you.

So, I want people to share my story. The reading of it will not be horrendous. I hope you can read it without too much cringing, but I want you to know that it damaged me. It caused emotional wounds, and it burned a hole in my soul.

I will admit it rears its ugly head every now and then bringing me to tears with the flashbacks. The memory of walking down that hallway in just my panties, frightened, not knowing what it was that I was afraid of. Standing naked by my father's bed, not remembering what just happened, makes it sometimes difficult to catch my breath.

What I want to say to anyone who has experienced any level of sexual abuse by anyone, is that your abuse is just as traumatic to your soul, to that inner child, as anyone's abuse. The details are irrelevant. You cannot compare them and say they are not as bad or as awful, or as horrendous as another victim's abuse. Those crimes have wounded you, altered you in some way, just as they have everyone else who has suffered at the hands of someone they loved.

Sexual abuse shatters our trust in the people or persons who have inflicted harm on us. The trauma placed us in a world that is no longer safe. The fear becomes part of our history.

The memories of that summer stayed with me for years even after my father moved out of our home that Christmas.

Even after he left, late at night I would imagine that I could hear his footsteps in the hallway heading my way. I always kept my bedroom door closed, trying to keep the monsters out, so when it would creak open from a breeze or for some unknown reason, I would freeze, terrified that he had returned.

And sometimes I was just frightened of the unknown. Filled with terror for no reason other than the fear already embedded in my heart.

As I grew up, I became very leery of men, of the men in my family. There were no more hugs, no more getting too close, and no more being alone with them. I felt that if I could not even trust my father, how could I trust any of them?

I lost a little bit of my happiness that summer. I was not that same gregarious child anymore. I was guarded and did not trust others. I did not feel safe in the world, my father's actions shattered whatever sense of safety I may have felt.

Chapter Eighteen

I WANT TO tell any victim who has been traumatized, one time or a hundred times that the abuse has affected your life too. It has left wounds on your inner self, your inner child. You have the right to feel betrayed, to feel violated, and to be angry and disgusted.

You have that right to witness those scars. You have the right to confront your perpetrator if they are still around somewhere. It might help you fight the demon inside. It might quiet the ghosts.

I remember that first episode of powdering. We laughed when he came in, thinking he was being silly. I remember asking him in my little child voice, "What are you doing in here, Daddy? What are you doing?"

And then him insisting on showing us how to powder our little bodies as if we did not know how to do it ourselves. The little particles scented the air, coloring things a little differently. We thought he was silly. We had used powder before. It was not something new. What pleasure did he get out of that little episode? I never really want to know.

We were oblivious to my father's sick intentions. We had no notion of where this was headed. We had no way to imagine the direction he was leading us. We just played along that first time because we loved him. We trusted him. "Go ahead," we said and laughed. "Show us how to put on the powder then. Go ahead, what the heck."

He powdered me. He powdered my sister. He powdered our little bodies, and we laughed at him. I did not feel threatened by my father that first time. I just thought, *Okay, you nut, get out of here, you silly head.* And then he left.

As an adult woman I think, *Did he go into his room afterwards and masturbate, the sick deviant?* I still have a lot of hate towards my father, but back then, I was blind to those kinds of deeds. I was unaware of his wicked schemes. I did not know what he was preparing to do or what he was up to. I hate him for shattering my trust, for the things he did to me. For the fear he left in that empty hole of my memories.

I know I have asked this question a million times, but how can a father look at their little child and feel lust?

What the hell is wrong in their brain that they can look at you and feel desire? Here is this skinny little girl, you can see the knobs in her spine, her thin little shoulders drooping under her T-shirt, she has no breasts, she has no pubic hair, there is nothing sexual about her physique. She has nothing: she is boney, her hair is rangy, and she is his daughter. How can he lust after this child?

I had no inkling that there were any sinister thoughts in my father's head. I did not have a clue what his real motive was in coming in and powdering our little bodies. Just remembering it right now brings tears to my eyes, and I am seventy years old. I did not know what kind of devil hid inside of my father. As a child, I trusted him completely.

Years later at my grandmother's insistence, I finally

went to see my father. She was getting older, and I wanted to make her happy. I wanted to show him that I was a strong person now, a stunning adult, and that I could look him in the eye after all these years without fear.

Shockingly, I discovered that my father had remarried and had two teenage stepdaughters. They lived in a cozy little house, he and his little family. All I could think of when I met them was: "What is he doing to those girls?"

I cut our visit short because I could barely stand being in the same room with him, fearing what awful things he might be doing behind closed doors.

I had flashbacks just being there. It disgusted me, the thought of what might be happening. I never went back after that night.

I cannot tell you their names, and I know they would not recognize mine because I never kept in touch with my father or his new family. I only hope that someone kept them safe from the demon hidden within him.

My father did not die at a young age, as he told us

he would that night he did whatever it was he did to me. Nope, he lived into a ripe old age. No cancer took him to hell.

My one consolation is that I know he is burning in some hellfire for the sins he committed, because no God would let someone like him go unpunished.

I want to tell any victim who might feel isolated, alone, that there are many who understand their pain. *They are not alone.* Sadly, the statistics show us that. I have been shocked by the number of women who have revealed that they, too, suffered at the hands of a parent, friend, or priest as a child.

By telling our stories, hopefully we will give courage to those who have yet to reveal their trauma, so that they too may begin to conquer their demons. Perhaps with enough talking we can get many of the victims to press charges if there is still time and bring these monsters to justice.

Remember, if you know of anyone who is molesting a child or adult, tell the world. If you are afraid you can do it anonymously: you do not have to give your name. Help the victims. Have these perverts and pedophiles arrested. Let the world know what kind of creatures walk among us. Often, these sick animals hide behind a friendly face and a kind personality. How do you think they build the trust we feel toward them? Make them pay for their crimes.

But the most important thing is to support these victims in their time of need. Help them feel safe in their world again. Help them tell their story out loud even if the words will shock and hurt you. The molestation or rape hurt them far more deeply than the words you will hear.

We can only heal if we push the demon out, we can only help others heal if we share our stories, and we can only help each other if we let the victims give voice to the harm that has been inflicted on their body and soul.

My father died at a ripe old age. I waited my whole life for him to die. I was deeply sorry it was not a short, painful death. As far as I am concerned, there are some people who do not deserve our forgiveness. Some individuals are just too rotten.

I personally would not want anyone to inflict harm on even these sick monsters, as they will surely be punished in the end. Do not punish yourself by seeking revenge, as their punishment will happen in this realm or the next.

As I said in the introduction: God give me the strength, courage and wisdom to tell my story, to give strength to others, and the courage for all of us to release our stories to the world. God grant me, God grant us, whatever it takes to free the child of her hauntings.

Epilogue

BACK WHEN I was growing up, there were no counsellors or counselling sessions available. Families hid their secrets behind closed doors.

As a child, I was not able to begin a conversation about the abuse I had suffer at my father's hands. I did not have the words to express my feelings or the knowledge of how to reveal what happened.

As children, we were innocent of the vulgarities of life. We did not have music videos or near naked men and women on television or in the movies.

People and families did not talk about sex. I learned about my "period" when my sister started her menses. The day I started bleeding my sister was the one to give me a Kotex and belt, to hold it in place. That was all the sex education I received.

Talks on pregnancy and sex never happened in our family. We learned from hearing other kids talking.

The only thing we ever heard from my mother when we were in our teens was, "You better not come home pregnant."

Now young girls are wearing skin hugging tights and shaking their booties to the current hits. And I am talking nine-year-old girls. It is very scary, as the statistics show.

When I first started hearing stories of rape and incest I was repulsed and saddened by the tales. Partly because it reminded me of my own trauma, but also because there were so many stories coming out into the open revealing that many children had or were suffering at the hands of someone they loved.

I never revealed my secrets. The abuse lay hidden, escaping in little bursts throughout my life, and that is the reason for this book.

I wanted to tell my story, and to encourage others to tell theirs as well. It is never too late to kill the demons, or at least put them to rest, no matter what your age. Writing this book has helped me tremendously.

I will admit as an adult to several sexual hang-ups, which I believe are the result of my molestation. My partner cannot tell me to take off my clothes. They can remove them, or I will remove them, just do not tell me to take them off. That is an immediate turn off. Do you suppose that is what my father did? Told me to take off my panties? How that child must have felt! People miss that part when they hear the stories, how we FELT when the abuse was happening.

I have never liked the lights on while making love. I feel too vulnerable, too naked. I feel as if there are unseen eyes staring at me, at my nakedness. It is as if a ghost is hiding in the barely lit room. Do you think that is why I like the darkness, so my father cannot see me?

Lubricants send me into a panic. Forget all those lovely, scented creams and things they have on the market today to enhance someone's sexual pleasure. They only sicken me. The thought of Vaseline or some type of goop applied to my private parts makes me cringe.

And I find tall men revolting. My father was six foot three. It gives me chills thinking about him. I look at a tall man and cannot even imagine a relationship with them. There is no attraction, no matter how good looking.

At times as an adult, I would choke up as the words tried to escape when there was talk of a child being molested or raped. I hated hearing that other children might be experiencing the same type of horror as I did.

Fear would wrap its ugly arms around me so that I could not speak, as I hid in a corner not wanting others to know my secret. Time allowed me to move forward. Life and its many responsibilities pulled me away from the ghost that tried to spoil my day.

Happily, I will admit that I have had a great sexual relationship for years despite all my baggage. Patience, kindness, and love were the tools my husband used to make that part of our relationship wonderful for both of us.

Even though the story inside this book recounts a sad part of my childhood, I want you to know that my life has been filled with great moments and wonderful adventures.

I have children and grandchildren that I deeply love,

and who love me.

In the past years, I have travelled to different parts of the world, and met some famous and interesting people.

Yes, the ghosts of that summer haunt me, bringing me to tears in my weaker moments, but I have learned not to let them cripple me. I have not allowed them to stop me from finding happiness in later life. I can think of so many more moments that bring a smile to my face with the remembrance. Bursts of happiness that brighten my day.

You, too, can create new, happier memories to carry into your adult life or later years. Do not let the abuse define who you are! Let it make you stronger. We are the bits and pieces of all the years lived, not just the individual moments.

Hopefully with talking, sharing, and communicating your trauma with others, it will help you put the ghosts to sleep. Help you to move your life in a new direction.

Do not continue to be a victim at the hands of anyone. Take charge of your life, find others to help you accomplish this goal. Write a book. Writing my story has helped me enormously. I think it would help you, too, even if you never want to show it to the world. You can let out the ghost and shoo it away. God bless and keep you safe. And as I always say in my blog, "Have **a GREAT** day today, **you and I deserve it.**"

Printed in Great Britain
by Amazon

27764361R00074